How Hand Washing Can Save the World

A Children's Disease Book (Learning About Diseases)

BABY PROFESSOR
EDUCATION KIDS

Speedy Publishing LLC
40 E. Main St. #1156
Newark, DE 19711
www.speedypublishing.com

How do you avoid getting sick? How important is hand washing in keeping you healthy?

Let's learn about the importance of hand washing as a way to avoid getting sick and to keep in good health.

Do you often touch interesting objects around you? What about holding a frog as part of a science experiment? Or playing ball games in the mud? The interesting stuff you touch can carry millions of germs that can easily transfer onto your hands. And then the next time you wipe your nose or touch your mouth, the germs can jump there.

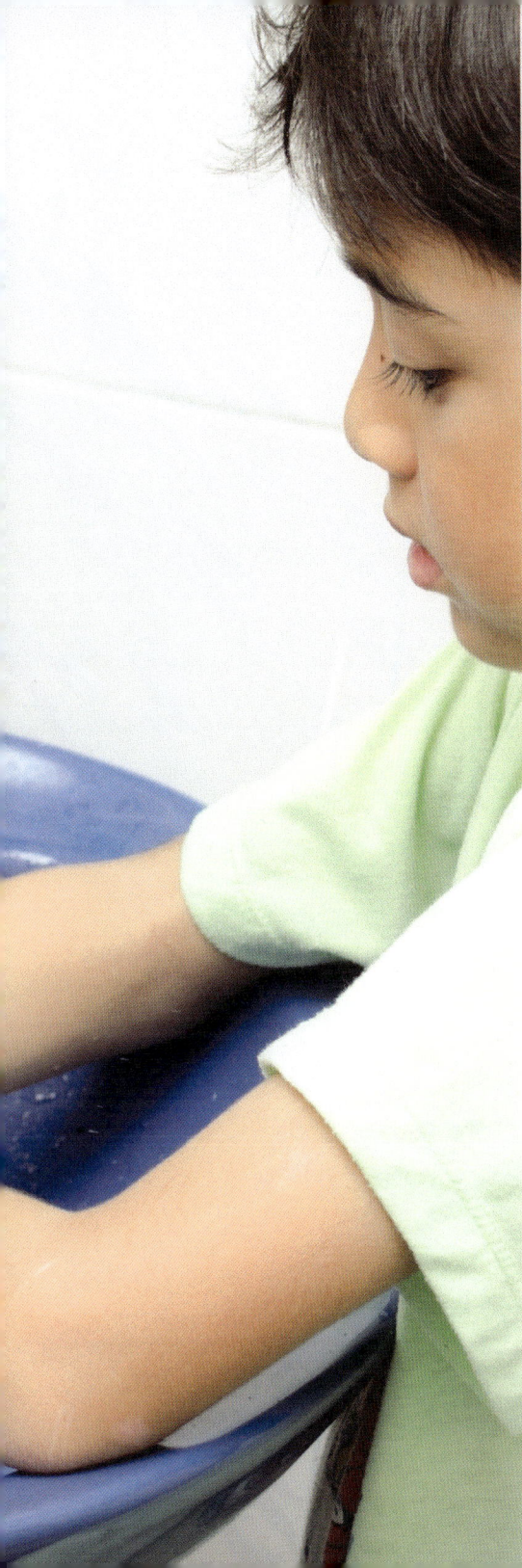

People keep reminding us to wash our hands, but still we find reasons to skip this basic daily habit. Maybe the water is too hot or too cold, or we're just in a hurry.

Germs and diseases can spread very quickly. Before we know it, the unwanted germs are already in our hands. Many health issues start and spread because we don't wash our hands with soap and clean water.

When germs get onto our hands, they can spread to the rest of our body and make us sick. Keeping our hands clean is an important move towards protecting ourselves from getting sick. We use our hands all day long, touching things that are dirty or that sick people have touched, so we have to keep cleaning our hands all day to stay healthy.

If we don't wash our hands before eating, and we touch our food, germs will get onto our food and then into our mouth as we eat. It is also possible to spread the germs to others.

Hand washing is very important. It is important to use soap since it removes germs more effectively.

Frequent hand washing keeps us away from germs and prevents infections. As we touch our eyes, nose and mouth, we can transfer germs into our body. Germs easily get into the body through the eyes, nose and mouth without us realizing it. We will only know of their presence once we are sick.

Unwashed hands can easily transfer germs to other objects and can make other people sick, as well. Germs multiply easily under certain conditions. As they transfer into food and drink, their numbers grow rapidly.

Proper hand washing will battle the germs, and will help keep you safe from disease. Hand washing is the simplest and most effective thing we can do to avoid diarrhoea, respiratory infections, and skin and eye infections.

People should learn the importance of hand washing, and how to wash their hands effectively.

Practice proper hand washing. Make it a healthy habit. Wash your hands properly before and after eating, after using the bathroom, after playing and when you've been handling dirty things.

Hand washing is one of the best ways to fight off germs, preventing them from spreading and keeping you and us from getting sick.

Good and proper hand washing does not take much time, and actually feels good. There is no reason to avoid washing your hands unless you really want to get sick. Make hand-washing a regular part of your routine.

You don't have to be a doctor to take steps to stay healthy. All of us can put up a very good fight against germs by washing our hands well, several times a day.

Nowadays, respiratory viruses are more contagious. Regular hand washing helps us to defend ourselves so viruses can't get out and spread.

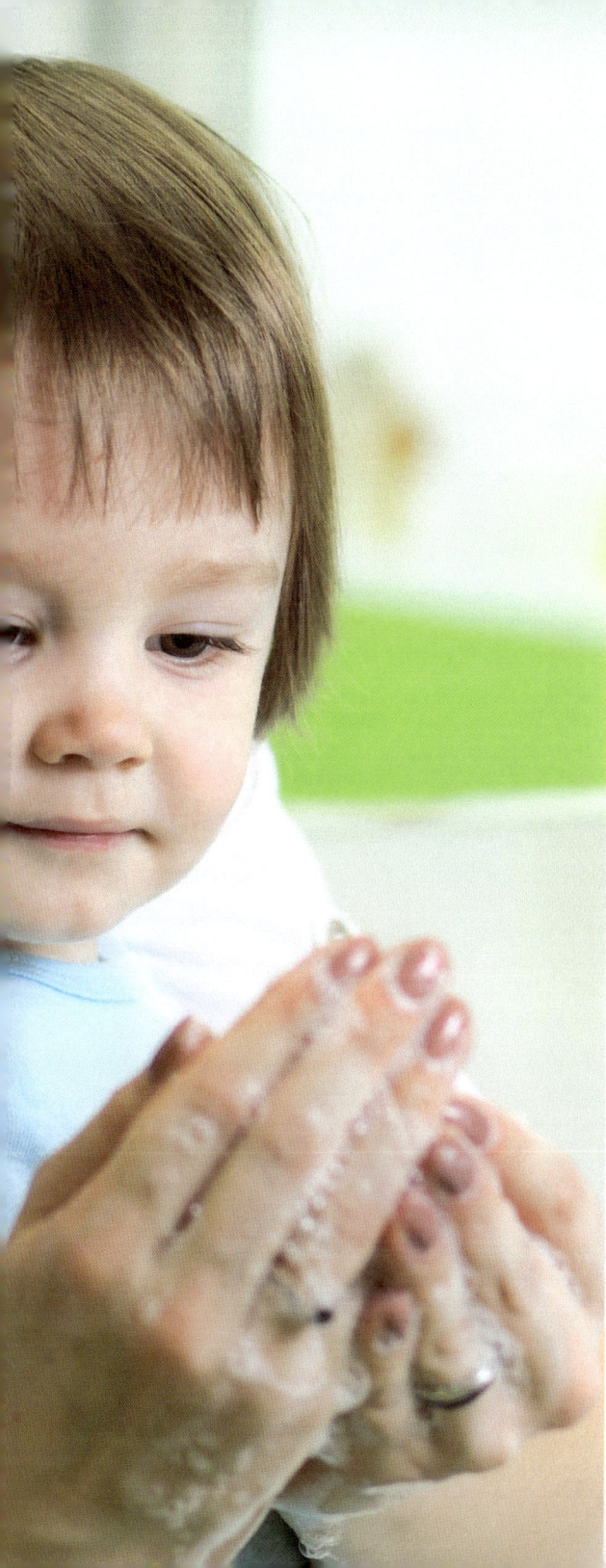

In summary, hand washing has three benefits. First, it saves us from infections from those around us. Second, it keeps us from infecting people around us. And third, it saves doctors' time and our money.

So now we have no excuse! The proof is clear that we should wash our hands more often.

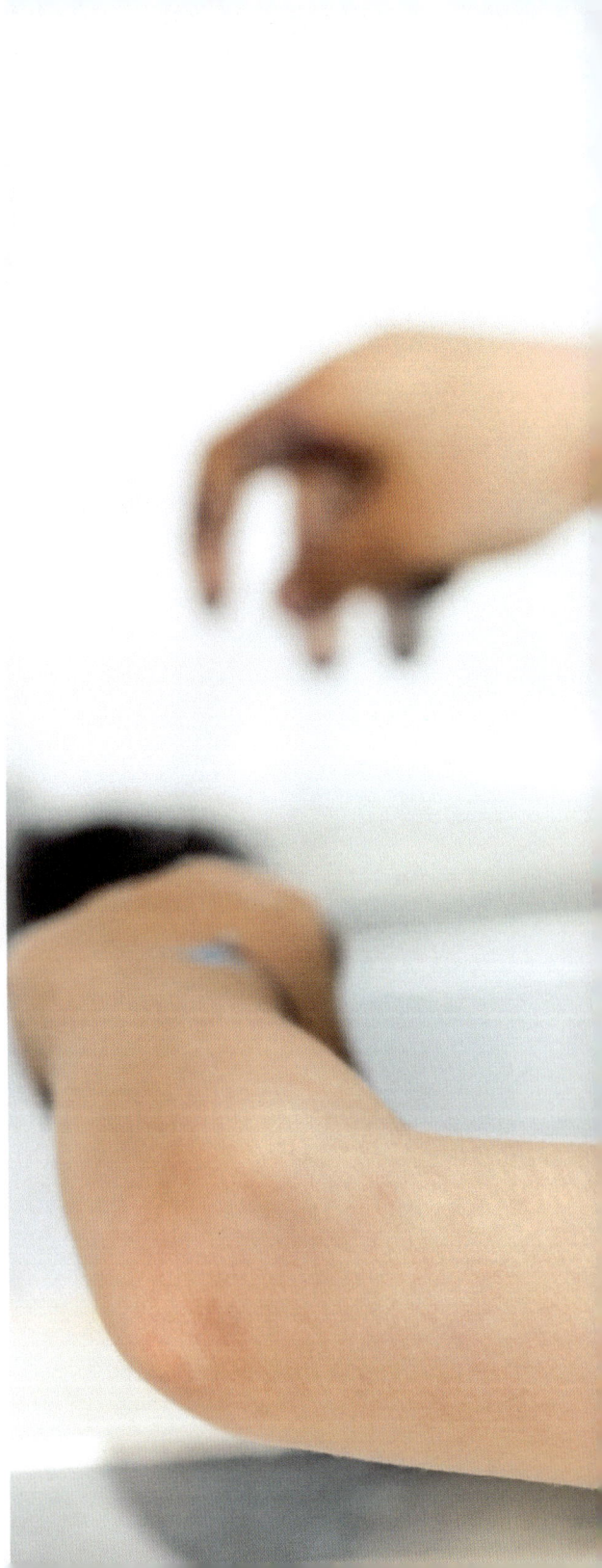

Visit

BABY PROFESSOR
EDUCATION KIDS

www.BabyProfessorBooks.com

to download Free Baby Professor eBooks
and view our catalog of new and exciting
Children's Books

Printed in Great Britain
by Amazon